The Book of Shi-Ji

Peter Maxwell Slattery

THE BOOK OF SHI-JI

Copyright © 2019 by Peter Maxwell Slattery

2nd Edition

Cover by Kesara (Christine Dennett), www.kesara.org

Editor: Jessica Bryan, www.oregoneditor.com

Published by Peter Maxwell Slattery

Email: petermaxwellslattery@outlook.com.au

www.petermaxwellslattery.com

ISBN 978-0-244-77062-4

This book is dedicated to all Beings throughout all planes and in between, throughout the universe, and beyond.

Thank You!

I am grateful to so many people, too many to mention them all by name. So I just want to say, "Thank you" to all those who have been my Guides, helpers, and teachers, and to everyone who has offered words of encouragement and supported me on my journey.

Also I would like to give a special thanks to my brother Ben and to Mum, Simo, Dad, Liz, and all of my very close friends.

I am grateful, also, to Jessica Bryan, my editor, and Kesara (Christine Dennett), who created the cover of this book.

Thank you also to the Beings who work with me, my Guides, the Orions, the Sirians, the Plejarens, the Star Nations, the Elohim, Michael, Metatron, my own God Self, Source, and last but not least, Shi-Ji.

Cheers!

Peter Maxwell Slattery

CONTENTS

The Book of Shi-Ji

INTRODUCTION

From November 24, 2014 to December 2, 2014, the (spiritual) Being known as "Shi-Ji" wrote through me everything that is written here. For those of you who don't already know about my story and Shi-Ji, here is a brief overview:

I am an experiencer from Albury N.S.W Australia, and I have filmed many crafts (what some of you would call UFOs). I have also had experiences with Beings from many different densities and places throughout the cosmos and beyond.

In December of 2010, I went public on primetime news on Channel 7 with footage I filmed in October 2010. This was followed by an appearance in 2012 on one of Australia's most popular morning shows, *Sunrise*, which is also on Channel 7.

Many people say my story is interesting because there have been many witnesses to the events that occur around me. To date, over one hundred people have witnessed unusual occurrences while in my presence, and some have gone on record about it. These events have included sightings of crafts, high strangeness activity, and sightings and interactions with Beings.

Now...the Being who wrote through me to produce this book calls itself "Shi-Ji." This Being originally appeared to me as a solid living person. Later, she showed me her true nature, and she is not a female or a human-type Being, at all. She is a Light Being.

It has also been revealed to me that Shi-Ji is from the Star Merope in the Pleiades, and that she is a gatekeeper there.

This book also contains messages from the other Beings who came through Shi-Ji while she was using me as a vehicle to write this book. I saw them in my Third Eye. The messages are from the Elohim, Metatron, The Councils, the Star Nations, and from races in Orion, Sirius, and the Pleiades. They were all familiar to me because I knew them from past experience.

Many of my interactions with Shi-Ji started out as seeing her in my apartment during the day, or when being told by telepathic communication to go outside to see her or her craft. All this continues to this day while I am in a conscious state, not in a dream state.

Later, the interactions became more intense, including meetings with her on her craft. Now she interacts with me at any time, not just by telepathy, but she also appears in my Third Eye.

Shi-Ji has spoken to me in my mind during my entire life, but I didn't know who it was until later. I simply heard a female voice in my head and didn't question it, because it never said anything that could be considered harmful. The voice always offered wise, positive advice.

Now...yes...she is not a human or a "she," but I still refer to this Being as Shi-Ji and as a female, because the human side of me needs a reference point to communicate what Shi-Ji has to say. It also gives others a reference point.

With all this said, a few other people have interacted with Shi-Ji, so don't be surprised if (with intent) your Guides, the Beings you work with, or even Shi-Ji come through while reading this book. After all, there is no such thing as a coincidence. You have been led to this information for a reason.

Please note that throughout the book, Shi-Ji uses the word "here" to refer to Earth. She also calls me "Pete." A

Glossary for some of the words that might be unfamiliar to some readers has been included.

I hope you enjoy these messages from Shi-Ji, which have been written in the way she first gave them.

Cheers!

Peter Maxwell Slattery

Chapter 1

GODS DO INTERESTING THINGS

As a facet of the collective, you have chosen to be here at this important (what you call) time on Earth. You are playing a very important part in the upgrade of humanity and in the evolution of the universe, in the overall scheme of things.

Humans and every other living thing on Earth, including plants, animals, and insects, have chosen to be here at this specific point in our own illusion. Nothing like it has ever been done on such a large scale before.

Beings from all over, inside and outside of our universe, are watching what's happening on Earth because the upgrade that is occurring is the grandest cosmic show of all shows.

Before a facet of you came here to partake in the human experience, you had many lifetimes during which you gained knowledge and had experiences that would enable you to handle this experience. Some of you have even been human before or lived inside the Earth, or just outside the frequency you are in now on Earth. Although the human experience is the greatest of all experiences, with it also comes the self-mastery lesson of all lessons. Everything has led you to this challenge.

You were warned about how hard your mission would be before taking up your contract, but you accepted it because of the importance of the mission. This "job" is for those who are in service mode.

Many behind the scenes (those you call extraterrestrials, or E.T.s) are your backup, your comrades, your fellow soldiers, although most of you are unaware of being with them in spirit. Even now, a facet of you is a part of the spirits you interact with.

Source—The God Source, Universal Consciousness, or God Consciousness, whatever you want to call it—had not experienced any other state before, so what happened was expected, meaning why things are the way they are. This occurred after the implosion and then the explosion of Source, which created the many manifestations of reality and the many planes of existence and inter-planes.

Many of you arrived here with amnesia, because your higher self and those you work with agreed it would be beneficial if you came in forgetting who you really are—and because the collective here lost the experience of Oneness long ago.

It had to be part of your mission, because you might not have been able to handle the human experience if you knew the true reality, but also because of the programming here. It had to be done in this way, because those who are part of the program would be able to manipulate you even more than you already are, and prevent you and the overall collective from completing your missions, which is to help yourself in the struggle against another facet of yourself in the bigger picture: the Archons (the Lower Light).

There is a positive and a negative aspect to everything. This is what occurred when Source decided to create all that is. Source also had to evolve beyond its pure state of love, before playing out what we are a part of now. So a part of the upgrade and growth of all is happening now.

As I explained to Pete a while ago, and as he already knew—and on some level as you all already know—this is how Source created the other planes and inter-planes.

In the beginning, there was a huge golden white light Orb (visual form of Source). It had never experienced anything except love, although it wanted to experience other realities and gain knowledge and have experiences. So it decided to split itself in two. As it did this, one-half exploded into zillions of spirits, and the other half expanded to contain the zillions of spirits, while keeping its resonant frequency.

When this happened, helper Beings were created, which you might call Angels. Each and every one of you (and everything that exists) is a part of the zillions of Beings that came from Source, and are Source, each a cell of Source.

With this said, to be able to handle the human experience, you need to have mastered and experienced many other states of being, such as being an animal, a plant, a rock, and more.

The only time this is not required is if you left Source recently and came to Earth when the call was given for help. In this case, because you had never left Source before, your higher self (which is a cell of Source) downloaded information from the lives and experiences of other Beings. This enabled you, the volunteer Being, to have the experience necessary to give the required assistance.

This is why when people claim they are Jesus or some other famous Being, they actually might be. So, yes, many could be telling the truth, because their program incorporates the program of Jesus or another well-known historical figure. The knowledge of Jesus (or whomever) was part of the program they needed in order to complete the service required.

This being the case, it is still hard to be here. Many have left and gone home, or let a walk-in take over their body computer, because being here is too difficult. Some have even taken the life of their own Earth body because it was too dense, limiting, and emotional, and because the mission was hard. It's not like Earth is their vibrational home—in spite of the many experiences that led to them calling it home. Earth does not vibrate at the higher state of Source.

When the life of the body has ended or a walk-in has been asked to come in, all parties must agree to the decision. This is how it works at the soul and oversoul level. So even though a Spirit has entered a body, if it can't handle life here, it can choose to leave.

In order not to waste the human body, another Being can come into the body and access all the necessary information about the life of the body, because the information about Earth life is contained within the programming of the body.

Also, you can go back to Source at any time because of the true nature of being in service mode. No matter what cell of Source you are, you can agree to come back later. Deep down you know this. So even if you decided to end your life or leave, you might decide to come back because of your service nature—even if you once agreed to a walk-in taking over your body.

Going back to the subject of leaving Source: you will slowly go through your experiences of being many other life forms (other than human) until you can handle the more complicated and limiting experience of being human. When you master being human, you become an Ascended Master, a Being of light, who can do whatever it chooses, because at that point you know the profound nature of all that is. You are in an unbounded state of consciousness and you are in service mode. You also understand Oneness and being an active part of it.

You have lived in many forms. You have been a plant, insect, bug, animal, and more, before moving on to more highly evolved life forms. The human experience is the most difficult, because it is a highly engineered experience created by the most advanced Beings throughout all planes. Humanity is a collective experiment within Source that was created for the physical plane. This had to be done.

In time, those who had done their walk here and moved on to the higher planes had to come back by reincarnation. This process was diverted to a recycle system here because of the Archon's program, which manipulates and recycles souls here, holding back the rest of the universe, and universes, from evolving as a collective. The Archons limit their own advancement and soul growth by creating a program that requires the energy of human emotion to survive.

The Archons are referred to in your Bible as the Fallen Ones. Due to misinformation—and because many of your ancient texts throughout many of your controlling limiting religions are being manipulated by the powers that be—the real information remains only in parts of your so-called teachings.

The Archons are known by many names throughout many cultures. Some know them as Jinn, or demons. There are many names for them, and there are many different types because of how they have evolved. Some look like what you commonly refer to as Greys (although not all Greys have an Archon nature). Others look human (or so they seem); some look like Shadow Beings or deformed foetuses; and some look like Reptilians. All of these Archons can shape shift.

They can appear however they want; they can trick you. They can manipulate you, and they are coming through now more than ever and showing themselves here because they are losing control and power.

Reptilians are believed to be the culprits behind the scenes of the control on your planet, but they have also been manipulated. They have been used as a shield, as a pushover, instead of the real culprits being found out, which are the Archons.

The Reptilian body is easier for the Archons to overshadow and manipulate than the human body; the Reptilians can easily manipulate the human body. This is why the Archons sometimes take possession of a Reptilian, because they can manipulate a human through them.

With this being the case, and because some of the Reptilians have been taking their power back in recent times, the Archons are directly overshadowing humans and committing psychic attacks now more than ever. They are almost out of every weapon in their arsenal needed in their fight to maintain control and power. So now they don't care about the wear and tear on their vibration, because they are trying anything and everything to survive.

Once the Archons were the Elohim (also known as the Anunnaki), but some of them wanted to go in a different direction. They wanted to play and manipulate other vibrations and be in *self-service* mode, so their makeup and structure also changed.

In present time, they rely solely on negative emotional energy from humans, animals, and even negative energy from ghosts and those who have not passed over, or who have tried but haven't succeeded. They have a grid around Earth in your solar system, which includes the Moon, Mars, Jupiter, and Saturn.

The grid is controlled by an artificial intelligence, which now controls the Archons. The grid runs their program because they created it. The program has a safeguard and a virus protector to protect the program from being bought down. You are the virus that was bought here to change their program, to help get the universe and beyond back on track. The Archons know this.

There is a frequency in your solar system that is trying to keep all of you under control. This is why higher vibrational Beings such as you, who are reading this, had to come back or come here and be part of the mission. You know how to handle the human body and manipulation here, because you have been here before or been given the necessary program. You have the tools to help humanity break free, which also helps the Archons and all Beings throughout the universe and beyond break free. What is happening here affects the evolution of all.

With the capability to recycle souls within the solar system, the reincarnation process in your universe has also affected the evolution of other universes. This will soon change, which is why all this is happening now.

The Archons are able of capturing, tricking, and recycling souls. They have been able to basically recycle their power source, which is negative emotional energy. In their ability to do this, they have been able to create many factions within the solar system to help contribute to their agenda by possessing other Beings.

Human bases under Reptilian (actually Archonic) control and Super Soldiers have the same technology as evolved Beings from planes beyond, all of which contributes to their control. They use

Reptilians, powerful families, and corporations as front men for their operations.

The Archons were able to do anything when they were in their original nature as the Elohim. They could create things by thought, but when they changed their vibration and went into *self-service* mode, this quality changed. They found it necessary to connect and create lower forms of technology, which are far less superior than the Elohim's today, because the Elohim do everything by thought. Still the Archon's technology far surpasses that of humanity, but not for long, because humanity doesn't know yet that they can also create by thought.

In truth, there is a war going on and all are a part of it. Those in the thick of it are completely unaware of it—meaning the masses of humanity. At this time, the Elohim are at the forefront of the war against a much more sinister force than the

Reptilians: the Archon network (which they once were).

Just like anything else, there are different levels and vibrations within the Archons, but not the Elohim, because the Elohim is a Creator Being state and it cannot become any more advanced at this time. However, the Elohim can fall, which has resulted in the Archons.

Really, what's going on is a war against your own self. Once you understand this and the true nature of reality, the profound nature of reality—which is that "All is One," and "What you do to others, you do to yourself"—then you will understand how everything is connected as one consciousness. Deep down you already know this.

You are God, a cell of God, and those who know this understand what is meant by "Gods do interesting things." Division and separation are illusions, and so is everything that is going on—except when you are in the plane of Source.

November 24, 2014

Shi-Ji via Peter Maxwell Slattery

Chapter 2

ANGELS, GUIDES, E.T.s, AND BEYOND

The concept of connecting to the God within is really an illusion, because you are already connected. It's just that on the physical, what you call the 3-D level, you have forgotten. This is part of the human experience, along with finding yourself again! Losing yourself and finding yourself is part of the human experience, and also the self-mastery experience.

Those who give you signposts, help, and advice (which you can take or not take), are what some of you call Spirits, E.T.s, Guides, Ascended Masters, Saints, Sages, and so on. When these Beings are not manipulated, their teachings throughout human history express this truth: what they can do, you can do, too.

At times there have been very active Light Cities, like those of the Brotherhood of Light. And, yes, even today, many Beings live right beside you in bases in your mountains, oceans, volcanoes, and under your homes in your cities and rural areas. Even though we are just beyond your frequency, sometimes those who choose to wake up are able to notice us. Although they might not be aware of us consciously, everything is happening for them on a higher level.

Portal areas have good vibrations, so most bases are near these portals because of the vibration. All of the portals are looked over by Metatron.

Each portal also has Ancient Beings that work with Metatron, along with the Guardians, which are connected to the Council of the Whole and under the vibration of the Elohim.

In Australia, for example, the ancients at the portal sites who work alongside Metatron and the

Guardians are Aboriginal Masters. Some of the Aboriginal Masters are so ancient that in addition to working in Australia, they also work at other portals around the world because they were located in other parts of the planet long ago.

In America, you have the Native American Indian Masters who work with Metatron and the Guardians because of their connection to certain areas. Ancient Tibetan Master Spirits work with Metatron and the Guardians in China, and ancient Indian Masters work with Metatron and the Guardians in India.

At this time, many of you are working (unknown to your conscious mind) in some of these areas, because you have certain abilities and can heighten the necessary energy needed.

In time, some of you will become aware of the work you are doing and the assistance you are giving and receiving from certain areas of the world, including from the mountains, rivers, oceans, and volcanoes.

Everything necessary is happening to help with the transition, and to help with the distribution of energy over Gaia and elsewhere, resulting from the vibrational change that is occurring. Because of the energy in the galactic plane, every planet in the solar system is being affected. From this, the energy causes the tectonic plates to shift, which heats up your oceans as the volcanoes are going off under them. Everything is heating up because of the change in energy, and one sign of this change is the exploding volcanoes. And it's not just happening on your planet.

The Sun has become more active with solar flares over the past twenty years, and it's assisting in the changes because it has also been abused as a result of the grid put up by the Archons. The Earth and the other planets and moons are also being abused by the grid, which has made humanity become the abusers to all in your solar system and, in effect, the universe and beyond.

Those you are interacting with at this time, whether subconsciously or not, are your Guides. They have agreed to work with one another. They are here to assist Earth with healing and to help the human race heal and reawaken, which will also help the overall collective in its evolution.

With this knowledge and realization, it is important to recognize that you and all Beings have free will and self-responsibility, and it's up to you to decide what you will do with it. We can guide and assist you, but you have the final say as to how to proceed. As Pete says, "Look at the fruit from the experience; that's how you can tell if the experience is what you perceive as positive or not." If your experience is of a positive nature, do what you will with it. If it is not, still do what you will with it—but know that anything that is in *self-service* mode is limited and can only develop to a certain point; whereas, being in service to others is unlimited.

You have left the plane of golden bliss (Source) to come down through the dimensions and have this physical experience, although you also have free will to go back to Source at any point. You can end your contract. And, like what we said in the last chapter, you can always come back to Earth when called.

A large number of those who left only had a certain mission, or they had to come back to finish their walk here because they were meant to have specific experiences. This was agreed on, not just for them alone but also for the whole, because all is one and one is all. Everything is interconnected.

You have many Guides. Some are in Spirit form; some are E.T.s; and some you cannot perceive.

They can be called on at any time. In calling them, notice the thoughts that come into your mind, because this is how your Guides interact with you, by thought—although many of you have doubt and think you are hearing only your own thoughts.

While you are in a human body (because of your mind chatter), you might have trouble noticing or believing the information that comes through from Spirit. The rule to go by is to accept the first thing that comes into your mind; deep down you already know this. Also, pay attention to any impressions, symbols, letters, and images you see in your Third Eye. Take notice of not only number synchronicities, but also any other synchronicities.

Because of programming, humans expect contact with Spirit Guides and E.T.s to be something it's not. The truth of the matter is that contact is happening all the time, but only some realize it. Those who believe these things are just a coincidence are missing the signs, although coincidence does exist if this is your programming. So if you think it exists, it does.

Through the study of quantum mechanics, many are realizing that the observer affects the experiments being conducted (this is related to Source experiencing itself). Many races with different agendas out in the cosmos are doing experiments within the human races.

So you need to understand that the preconceived notions and the belief system of the observer can affect outcomes. Therefore, the outcomes are going to fit their agenda.

We, your Guides, are here all the time. We work in sync with each other for the collective through the Council of the Whole at the higher planes, and with the different committees of the Star Nations, Galactic Councils, and Federations. We use these terms as a reference to assist in your understanding.

Through number synchronicities, take notice of your thoughts, because at times they are not your thoughts. They are projected to you from your Guides to help lead you to your tailored experience in your current reality. Number synchronicities are a signal to take notice of your thoughts. This is the main way we communicate with you—through thought. This is done in a way so as to not disrupt you too much or harm your body computer, which is being programmed in a certain way.

With regard to number synchronicities, just take notice of your thoughts when you become aware of them, or when you think about what you were talking to someone about, or what you were listening to at the time the number synchronicities occurred. Synchronicities are a sign for you to take action or research something (which you will be guided to do anyway), or they are a confirmation about how to go about something. The sign will confirm your thoughts.

You are at the forefront of the experience here, and we are here to help you behind the scenes. The Archons are doing the same thing (although in a negative way), playing out their agenda in your realm behind the scenes. So we must do the same thing, which we all agreed upon due to Universal Law, although the Archons have broken that Law and now things need to be rectified.

Any civilization that is more advanced than those it comes across cannot openly interfere with Universal Laws. If they do interact, there are limits and a certain way that is allowed. Universal Laws do not allow any civilization to be affected by another in a disruptive way, because all Beings and races have a right to develop spiritually and technologically at their own rate. However, this only applies if those who are the higher civilization agree to the illusion. The Archons have not agreed, and they have infiltrated in a way that is not so noticeable. They hide behind the Reptilians, and the Reptilians hide behind their human vessels.

This situation has occurred because all of those who are not part of the Archon agenda and network had three options: (1) do nothing; (2) reincarnate and play a part in humanity at this very exciting time; or (3) help behind the scenes, which is what is happening during a lot of UFO sightings. These sightings include many crafts of both a positive and negative nature.

At this time, by agreement, many of you are catching up with what some of you call your Star Families. All of you have been many Beings before, and the Beings you interact with much of the time have been, too. They are your friends, family, Guides, and even other facets of yourself. Yes...some of them are other facets of you interacting with yourself—in the same way that we are all one consciousness interacting with itself.

Seeing things like this shows how all is connected, and how all is known and can be known by anyone who practices the awareness of Oneness and thought.

You can call upon and connect with your Guides through thought, or get your own information by jumping ahead and accessing whatever you desire, whether in the past, present, or future— because all is happening at the same time.

Your governments know this, but even they have been controlled in their attempts to access information. They are limited in the information they can get from the method known as remote viewing. This method shows a glimpse of what can be achieved. The remote viewer and the information they receive are limited because they do it in a linear way involving a certain format and process

The true process of remote viewing involves *not* writing down the information. It is merely downloaded into the mind of the viewer. "What's the first thing that comes to mind?" That's it! This is how remote viewing and communication across all dimensions and all types of Beings is done—by thought!

The Archon network manipulated remote viewing in a military way because they were on to it. The masses have also been misled, just as the messages from the Saints, Sages, and Masters throughout the history of humanity have been manipulated.

The fact is that you are God, and the Guides and E.T.s you interact with are, too. All is a cell of God. All together, we make up God. It's just that the experience here has been set up for you to slowly understand the true nature and reality of God so you are not shocked too much by the enormity of what's going on as a result of manipulation. When you are not in the body, all this is easy to fathom because you are unbounded and part of all that is.

Call on your Guides, connect with them, and realize that some of your Guides are different facets of you, and that in the end everything is one consciousness. Work with your Guides and know they love you.

Just take your time when directing your intent to connect with your Guides. Block out those who are not in line with your mission and take notice of your thoughts—your environment, what you see, hear, and feel—because your Guides are with you always. All you need to do is make an effort to increase your awareness of them.

November 25, 2014

Shi-Ji via Peter Maxwell Slattery

Chapter 3

THE SELF-MASTERY EXPERIENCE

Besides being on Earth in service mode and being workers of light, during this time of the biggest changes throughout all planes and universes you are also here for the human experience, because it offers the most lessons of all! With it comes not only the illusion of separation, but limitations and high emotions, as well. These are illusions. The lesson here is to be able to overcome all limitations and see everything as it is.

You have not been disconnected from Source; you have not been kept in the dark; you have not been cast aside; you have not been forgotten; and you are not lost. You have only been distracted from the real reality by the illusion.

Realization of distraction, once truly recognized, along with the reality that you are a cell of Source, will allow you to manipulate your facet of reality because you know everything is an illusion. It all starts with a thought!

The many races, including those from Sirius, the Pleiades, Orion, Arcturus, Lyra, Andromeda, and the Reptilians, Mantis Beings, the Elohim, and many others— including the different densities of races from the same places—have embraced the collective goal to create a super being in the 3-D realm. However, what came about was unexpected. Everything is actually part of the upgrade, and now humanity is going through an upgrade, too. Everything throughout all planes, the universe, and beyond is being upgraded.

Many wonder why they look like the Beings they interact with (meaning two arms, two legs, and so on). Well...this is because you are us, a mixture of us, and you are continuing the program because the different races on Earth are mating with one another. Getting back to Oneness, in time you will regain the abilities you lost when you separated from the state of Oneness long ago. These abilities have been lying dormant within you.

You must master your emotions and thoughts while you are in the body and having the human experience. Once this is done by enough of you, the collective will be affected and it will be easier for the rest to do.

Many of you are directly from Source and the higher vibrations, and you have come back down to this realm. When placed around the Earth as you are, an energy grid is created.

This affects everything! Those between you, near you, above, and below you are all being affected, but a lot of you don't know it. Many humans want to know their place. However, the reality is that a large majority of you have come here just to be here.

By your presence, you are affecting and playing a part in the healing of the Earth, and the healing and awakening of the human race. As an extra bonus, while you are here you also get to master the human experience, which is the experience of all experiences! Yeshua, Moses, Muhammad, Buddha, and all the Saints, Avatars, and Sages have been similar messengers.

From here, you can activate your light body and connect with your multidimensional self, your Merkabah, and experience different light spectrums as being one at the same time, because when you connect with your higher self you are unbounded.

Yeshua, Muhammad, Moses, Ezekiel, Buddha, and many others have done spiritual work here on Earth. They also worked in many other places, before going back to Orion, the Pleiades, and elsewhere to reconnect with the Orion Council of

Light, the Elohim Councils, and many other types of Councils. They are in service mode, and you are also playing your part in doing service.

No "self" is recognized when in service mode because you *are* the Oneness. This is what you do in the Oneness state of awareness, because your true nature and program are Oneness.

The evolved ones who have done their walk automatically go back to Orion, the Pleiades, and so on, because their experiences and missions are complete. Then they create new missions, with the understanding that love is the key to all this. Other races from far and beyond experience love, but not like humans—unless they are at Source, they are a Master, or they are in the state of unboundedness—because the human state has emotions like no other. However, the intensity of love in humans is not the same as within Source.

No organism can equal it, which is why many of you might like sex, due to it being close to the state of bliss you feel when you are unbounded or at Source. Mastering your sexual feelings (which are an illusion) is also part of the self-mastery lesson here.

We are not suggesting you avoid sex, but rather that everything should be done in moderation, within reason, and coming from a place of love—and without ego and jealousy.

The experiences and lessons that lead to self-mastery and then to service mode are not done just for the sake of it, but rather for the love and passion in acting from a place of love and service. Self-mastery leads to the state of being in service mode.

Ego is one of the main programs that can stop you from reconnecting with the God within, but ego can be broken. It's a distraction that produces emotions that must be mastered in order for you to see the illusion of separation for what it is, an illusion. Ego divides, which is what the Archons want.

Ego is the reason for the Tower of Babel (as described in your Bible), which led to the separation of humanity and loss of the experience of Oneness, and the ability of humans to understand each other. Ego is the reason the Archons manufactured royalty and a social structure and, in a smart way, they got the go ahead by the masses. This did and still does contribute to the power of the Lower Lights. It's a front, like the Reptilians being in control of the manipulation when it is really the Archons. Ego is the root of human difficulties, but it was engineered this way. Ego divides countries, states, towns, and people, and there is much that can be learned from it.

Like the yin-yang, balance is one of the key components in ascending and reconnecting with the true nature of self and all that is. Balance of family life, social time, time with your partner, time by yourself, and exercise—everything is about balance. From a state of balance you can excel exponentially. In order to be productive, healthy, spiritually connected, and happy, balance is the key.

What most humans don't realize is that by being here they must learn to walk in two worlds. This is part of the self-mastery human experience, and one of the hardest things to do.

When humans start to wake up, they realize the illusion and see the manipulation for what is. Then they think they have it all worked out, only to find out how deep the rabbit holes goes. They try to project their reality onto others—which is worse than what those who are controlled by the

Archons do—because they have an idea of the real reality, and those who are manipulated do not.

With awakening, you will begin to learn the lesson of self-mastery and letting go. You will learn to judge only yourself, not others, and then later on to not even judge yourself. Everything starts with you.

We are not trying to judge the others that we write of here. Rather, we are pointing out that the so-called awakened ones (when starting to awaken) judge others, even though they don't want to be judged themselves. They are doing that which they are trying to stop from happening.

Simply judge yourself instead of others, because when awakening you have more responsibility. Even then, you should not judge yourself because it is also a distraction. Most of all, you need to observe your sensations and thoughts.

You see...the more you know, the more you recognize. You will see the real reality slowly for what it is: a process. You cannot be fully enlightened until you have done your walk and are connected fully back with Source. This being the case, being in both worlds at the same time and having a balance between them needs to be recognized—in both worlds.

What we mean by this is that when some awaken, every waking moment is spent researching and listening to others, rather than trying to connect and follow their own journey to discover their own information (which is going to come to them anyway). In this type of situation, sleep, health, and relationships are affected in a way that can be damaging. Sadly, most go through this and, in time, they find a balance. The process is their journey. It's what they must do on their walk here.

Again, finding a balance between this world and the spiritual world is the main requirement, because you must have pure balance in both worlds. You are here to bring the spiritual reality through to the physical reality, and vice versa. There must be pure balance, because you are here in the first place, which is to play a part in the evolution of humanity. In order to do this, you need your own connection to the spirit world.

Whether subconsciously or not, many of you just let things be how they are, because you are mainly energy workers who do not consciously know too much—even though you have Starseed traits and you are interested in healing, the paranormal, UFOs, and many other subjects.

You are all energy workers, although most are not aware of it. However, you don't need to be, because this is your job while you are here. You are Undercover Energy Workers, and the purpose of your higher selves has been hidden, even from you.

Doing energy work and holding the energy here is important, because we all need to help contain the energy for what is already happening and will continue to happen in the future.

You can be the most effective by maintaining your balance between both worlds. You will learn the most and have the most fun and exciting times.

You are here to help, and you can only do it when you are connected. You might be unaware of being an energy worker, and this why some of you have been led to this book. "As above, so below." You manifest this reality here, too.

The main point is to work on yourself, find your own connection, and have confidence. Yes...the human mind has been conditioned over time to create doubt. This is part of the Reptilian traits that were given to the human body computer. This is a distraction. Anything with distraction and hierarchy is an illusion. It does not come from a place of love and service. It is a distraction.

For this to be realized, you need both yin and yang. No one is above or better than anyone else, even with the Councils and so on. Everyone decides and does what they do best—this is how it works everywhere else! We do what we love and are passionate about because this is the best way we can help others.

Even if we are not the best at something, we have the opportunity to learn about a subject and master it because we have passion about that particular subject.

We all support each other in these decisions. Even if you are not the best at something, you are supported anyway, because of your passion for doing what you are good at.

Captains on ships do this because they are best designed in their reincarnation of this facet of their life for the particular job of being a captain. Likewise, pilots are best suited for their assigned job. The scientists and diplomats on the Councils, who communicate with one another, do what they do because they are good at it.

Many races embrace what they are good at, but unfortunately many humans do not. Humans are programmed from an early age to help strengthen and contribute energy to the energy grid created by the Archons. Fortunately, this is breaking down.

For self-mastery to be effective you must work on yourself. Over time, this will be projected outside of you and manifest in the reality it is directed towards.

All you can do is work on yourself, and the collective will do the same. As more achieve self-mastery, more will become Masters—although when unbounded you are already all Masters. You just need to realize that when you are in a human body, you can be a master, too. It's up to you.

November 26, 2014

Shi-Ji via Peter Maxwell Slattery

The Book of Shi-Ji

Chapter 4

IT'S ALL ABOUT LESSONS AND EXPERIENCES

What you call life is about gaining as much knowledge and having as many experiences as possible. Life is about experience. All this goes into what some call the Akashic records, and it also goes towards Source understanding itself.

Much of what occurs while in the human mind cannot be comprehended unless you are in a meditative state. A higher level of consciousness is needed to evolve, and you can get to this state through having experiences and developing greater awareness.

When someone treats you badly, or you treat someone else badly, learn from it. Those who have a greater understanding of reality understand that when you do wrong to your brother, you are doing wrong to yourself. This is the reality of the situation when you see God in everything. You are God and so is everything that exists. It doesn't matter whether it is a material object or not. If you think something has consciousness, it does, because everything is made from a cell of Source.

"Treat others as you want to be treated," has been a common saying on Earth for a long time, but it is still not being put into practice, as it should be.

When someone does wrong towards you, try to understand what you can learn from it. When you do to others what you would not like done to you, learn from that, too. Know that you don't die, and no matter what happens you will always be safe. Don't worry if your ego is beaten while you are having the human experience. See it as a lesson, a time for growth and learning more about self-mastery.

With all this said, also know when to stand up for yourself and your fellow beings, because this can be a lesson in courage. Over many thousands of years, on and off on Earth, many humans have lost this quality. This is why some have not stood up for others and their own rights. The illusion of punishment, what others think, and even acceptance have caused this loss.

Know that you need the acceptance of no one else. Accept yourself, because the God within (which is a cell of all) loves you unconditionally no matter what you do. Understanding omnipresence is the key!

The illusion of separation has been programmed into the human experience. You are the virus sent here to get rid of the Archon virus (the Archon network) and move on. Then all will be able to evolve in the bigger body, which we will call Super God Source. This is your universe, and all the other universes are a part of it, too. Only a few have seen the other universes while in the human body and mind. When having the human experience, it is hard to absorb the vast enormity of it all, knowing that the Super God Source is a part of something even bigger.

Shedding and losing the beliefs of others, your own beliefs, and the programs of separation, is one of the most important things you will do while you are here. We know it is hard, because only the Gods that chose to come here to help had the courage to do so. They had drive and purpose and they were in service mode. Understanding this, you will know that being here is and was not ever meant to be easy.

Even when phasing in and out of densities, planets, stars, and the inter-plane between everything contained within your Merkabah, a trade-off has to take place. Nothing dissolves or disappears; it just changes state. Everything thing is energy, and to understand this you need to understand that energy cannot disappear. It can only change state. Just like when you are connected and using your light body (your Merkabah), you don't float and fly around all the time. You pop in and out of where you want to be by thought and thought energy transfer, because when you are connected you can understand energy transfer and how all is one. You can be connected with other particles anywhere in space and time.

Your scientists know that when any two particles are separated, they still have a conscious connection. This means you can manifest anywhere, anytime, through thought. When you know this fully, you will know every particle is you—another facet of you on a larger scale—and everything is a cell of Source and connected.

You will be able to walk, fly, or whatever you want to do in your light body after you have been teleported, or what seems like teleportation has occurred. You will also be able to manipulate matter because you understand Oneness, and you know that all you are doing is manipulating yourself. This is also part of the self-mastery experience for the cell of Source you are using to have this experience.

Many of the lights in your sky are advanced Beings. Some are in service mode; some are in *self-service* mode. The ones you call Masters (you are one, too), are floating around in their Merkabahs after being teleported to this plane. When they are in their Merkabahs, many Beings can join as one or separate, and they can do whatever they want. Those who see and experience this are having experiences on a super-consciousness level. In this state, you will be able to communicate with your family, friends, and fellow Beings from other planes— Beings that are other facets of yourself.

Those who use crystals or metals (what some would call nuts and bolts) for their crafts are also trying to get to the mastery state, even though they are a lot more evolved than those in your public domain at this time.

Although they have a conscious connection to their crafts (a symbiotic relationship) and can navigate in a way similar to the way we do, they are still using a lower form of technology. Consciousness is the best and most advanced technology. When you know this, anything can be done by thought...yes...just a thought. This is part of the self-mastery experience, and doing it while in a human body is the ultimate achievement. The real reality is that humans can do anything.

Add your cell, your Being, your name, to the names of Masters. Eventually, you and all Beings will go fully back to Source and start over again, like cell regeneration. Yes...once this huge cycle ends, everything will start over, but the same mistakes will not take place. New ones will be made, which Source individually and as a collective with other universes will have to experience in order to evolve and grow again. For us, this means another all-new self-mastery excursion through the planes. Everything is a part of this ongoing evolution.

When tested during the human experience, ask yourself: *Why is this happening? What can I learn from this? Is something else at play here?*

Sometimes it is necessary to just sit back and let things play out. With Pete, we had to keep telling him, "Go with the flow." No one can control everything. Even Source has to go with the flow.

When you are unhappy or you have impure, negative, or self-serving thoughts, thoughts about doing things you know are wrong or anything else you do not want to be thinking, ask yourself, *Are these my thoughts or someone else's?* Then ask your Guides, the Beings you work with, and your higher self to help you get rid of energies, Beings, and psychic bonds that are not in line with your highest purpose. Ask that they be healed, evolved, and moved on to a better place. This is important.

Often, we put our power, future, and happiness in someone else's hands, when we are actually the masters of our own destinies. When we are not in this state, we still need these experiences, because it has been agreed to at a higher level. Once we recognize this, the next phase of evolution in the human self-mastery experience will unfold.

Many of those who walk in the Lower Light, meaning the Archons, will try and put roadblocks in your way. These are signs you are doing what you are supposed to do. Just know the big lesson is self-responsibility. You decided to have the illusion of separation when you came here.

When you have negative thoughts you know are not yours, send them back to where they came from with love and light.

The Lower Light manipulates many who are here at this time. They talk about love and light, although they do not recognize it in their current state. What we mean by this is they chose to ignore their lessons. They are not open to new experiences and growth. They say, "That's negative," when you bring up the subject of the Lower Light, even though we are at war with ourselves here. To be affective, you need to understand both sides.

In the end, negativity is only what the observer perceives as negative. Those who are doing good are perceived as negative to those who perceive good as bad. It's all about your perception of the illusion.

The basic fact is this: as a collective, we are trying to manifest the state of Source— its unbounded original state—in the other realms it created within itself.

Do not judge others unless you have walked in their shoes. Even then, you still should not judge, because your personal past and past life experiences affect how you react to situations. All of us must do our walk here, and sometimes some people do not want help on a higher level because this is part of their walk.

You cannot spiritually highjack someone or manipulate and affect another person's spiritual advancement and journey, which is why sometimes you must sit back and simply let things be. Turn the other cheek! Each will know from thought (the information coming from his or her higher self) when this needs to be done, because it has to be done on a case-by-case basis. Just know this: you cannot spiritually affect another person's journey. This is why some of you get blocks on people.

Patience is another issue you need to deal with here on Earth. Wherever you came from and wherever you have been, you didn't need to experience patience like you do here. The illusion of linear time and laws, and many of the restrictions humans have placed on themselves, require patience, although this is part of what has been agreed to at the higher level. Everything here has been created by Source to be experienced.

Balance is again a key, with respect for the temple (the human body), which only houses a facet of who you are when you are here for the human experience. From what is sprayed in your air to what is put in your food, and to what substances many of you smoke and put into your body, many of you are in difficult situations, but these situations were agreed to by your higher selves. Through self-respect, will, and spiritual power, you can overcome these things.

Much can be achieved through the vibration of thought. Many of the keys and signs of this are not just given in the master teachings. They can also be found in some of what we have created in your fields (which you call crop circles).

Through thought, sound, and vibration, you can change your reality. As a collective, there needs to be a balance between technology and spirituality. You can heal yourself, when necessary, and prevent all diseases and cancers, because you are able to manifest whatever you need in a subconscious state in the body computer. From consciousness to light, to sound, and to matter, you are and have experienced all.

The real reality of it is to know you are light and you are consciousness, and that all is one consciousness.

November 27, 2014

Shi-Ji via Peter Maxwell Slattery

Chapter 5

COMPASSION, LOVE, AND GRATITUDE

In order to evolve and be in service mode, we must have compassion, love, and gratitude for self, above all others, especially when we are experiencing the illusion of separation.

You are in a pure state of love when you are in your light body. But when a facet of you is experiencing dense physical reality, your Being, your cell, is screaming to become light again and manifest the state of love in the physical realm. The goal is to achieve both.

Before we, as a collective, let the experiment go too far, we decided we must experience your reality, so we reincarnated as you. However, your body could not handle our energy, which is why, over time, we created another hybrid.

Some of you call the hybrid offshoot body the Nephilim. We created many types of Nephilim because, as the project evolved, so did the body. These bodies were able to handle the intense energy more easily.

As this experiment become more intense (as it is now), we could only evolve the body so much in order to handle higher energy. So before coming to this plane, all of you split up a facet of your spirit and only put part of it in the human body. Gradually, as the human body and the light body adapt to the changes, and as the physical body and light body gets tweaked from energy work (in order for it to handle more energy), more spirit will come in from the facet of spirit you originally split away from.

The splitting up from one facet of spirit was also needed because all of you have high energy. It also had to happen because those who are here now have the highest state of Christ consciousness, although they are unaware it until they are awakened.

Love is instilled in you all. It's up to you to decide how to experience your reality and what vibration you would like to be in. One option is to be like kids, who live in this reality with love. You can be amazed and excited by the unknown, just as they are. The other option is to be negative and fearful, scared of the unknown, because of your need to be in control.

The only thing that holds you back from evolving, when experiencing the illusion of separation, is you. Everything that holds you back is you.

Look carefully at how you react to events here. Do you assume outcomes of a negative nature, and when something arises that is unexpected do you immediately perceive it to be negative? When a negative thought comes to mind, analyse the reality of what you are experiencing and see what you can learn from it. Is your reality really that bad?

Sometimes when negative things happen, your higher self or those you work with planned the events in advance to steer you in the direction you need to go.

To move forward from this way of thinking, you must first notice how you react and what you are thinking. If you desire change, it will manifest—if it's in line with your mission and your intentions. A lot of people want to change but they don't want to do the work, or they get scared of the unknown.

When manifesting a loving and peaceful life, you will be tested on every level. You will experience life's ups and downs, because everything will be thrown in front of you in order to test you. This is just the way it is.

The more you wake up, the harder it will be, and you will be tested more than most because you see more than most.

For you to evolve and change, you must first love yourself, understand yourself, and grow in this way. You must love yourself. Understanding others will help you; judging others will not. The main thing is to work on yourself and understand yourself.

You affect your reality through your actions and your spirit, your higher self, by bridging the gap between realities and connecting with all facets of yourself, and by understanding the God Cell of yourself. This is the way it works.

Once you start to work on yourself, and you have compassion and gratitude for your experiences and all that is, a tipping point in terms of evolving and experiences with the all-knowing part of yourself will happen. From there, service mode will come into play more than ever, because this is what happens when all these things are done. You attract that which you seek.

Even if what you are trying to achieve seems impossible, understand that what you are trying to manifest into reality is already happening. Believe that it has actually happened. You attract that which you seek.

When thinking of something positive and then it happens, understand that you made it happen. Again, just like your scientists who talk about your experiments being affected by those who conduct the experiment (the observer), in the same way, you are actually affecting the outcome—unless on a higher level something else is at play, which some call divine intervention.

Sometimes, there will be negative influences, and with this comes an experience for you to have love and compassion for the Lower Light, too. No one can be left out, because all is one. Once you see God in all, you will have love and compassion for all, and with this comes gratitude for all.

There will be times when you will be tested. This is exactly what challenges are: tests to see if you are ready for the next level, the next experience, the next stage in your journey; this is what they are. It's up to you as to whether you can handle the situation and your experiences before you go to the next stage.

When you are in the state of unconditional love, gratitude and compassion, the thoughts that once held you back from evolving will no longer matter. Everything that once mattered, petty things, will matter no more. What people think, do, and say, will not matter. Technology will not matter, and the negative things that hold you back will not matter, because you are at a different vibration when coming from a place of love.

From free energy, to food and shelter for all, to everyone having everything they need, this is what happens when you are coming from a place of love and vibrating at a higher level of consciousness. In this state, you are in service mode and so is everything that vibrates with you.

You have all been in this state before; it depends on which level you want to go to at this time. At the lower levels of higher consciousness, deterrence is still possible, along with jealousy and hierarchy. These are tests. What vibration are you ready for? It's your decision! When you are connected to your Source self, there is no judgment, and it's up to you what you want to do with what's revealed each time you reach a higher level of consciousness.

You and those you work with have agreed on your paths. The signs of this are there, which some might call coincidences. Everything is already set up. Just go with the flow, go through the motions, and accept whatever happens.

Time and time again, many have come back here, whether because of the manipulation or because they chose to on a higher level. Many have seen a glimpse of what you would call Peace on Earth, although it's always lost due to losing the Oneness. The Mayans, the Native Americans, The Australian Aboriginals, the Africans, the Japanese, the Chinese, the British, all of these cultures have not achieved what they seek because of being divided, and because of intention and searching outside of themselves for answers and happiness.

All cultures could have prevented themselves from being over taken by another culture, if they had the Oneness, because when you have Oneness, anything that goes against your will cannot manifest into your reality.

All cultures have had small groups or individuals achieve a higher vibration, although as a collective you have not for a very long time. Only when you have unity as a collective and understand Omnipresence, and be it, will you achieve Peace on Earth again.

In time, you will wake up more and empower yourself more. Only you can do it. Bit by bit, you will start to see your journey for what it is and connect with the people you have planned to do so with on another level.

You will attract the people who are harmony with you and you will also get everything you need, because this is what happens when you are doing what you are supposed to and you are coming from a place of love. The starting phase seems hard. It's like anything you start, because the illusion of fear, of change, and of being out of your comfort zone make you feel like change is too difficult.

Due to what's in your genes from the experiences of your ancestors, your lineages—through which you are being affected—you are here now reading this at this time as a reminder that you are the bravest and you made the decision to come here. You are the only ones who can handle the situation. You have either done your walk here before, or you have been given the program to handle existence here. Because of your evolution, you are the only spirits that can create change by playing a part in humanity, which, in turn, helps humanity to help itself.

From addiction to attitudes, to all that is, everything is testing you and has been instilled in you from your ancestors. This is all being cleared up now!

"Cleaning up your baggage," does not mean just the baggage from what you create here, it's also about cleaning up the baggage for those who came before you, your linage, and also as a collective.

Because of your bravery and your nature, you have chosen to clean up baggage like never before, even as the manipulation is trying to keep you down. Everything is being thrown at you to distract you from your mission and from reconnecting with Source, although you are getting through it.

Realizing that conditions here are like never before, you can create change like never fathomed before, while you are in the human body and having the human experience.

Just for fun, you have chosen the most deeply amazing, fruitful, and rewarding, learning experience—not just for you as a cell of Source, but for Source itself, which encompasses all. You are the bravest.

With positive thinking, you can do your work. You know this; nothing here is new; you already know all this. It's just that you are being reminded because of the veil put over you by the vibration here, which is trying to keep you down. You are here to bring the higher energies in.

Positive thinking and projecting positive energy into your food and water, and into everything you do, makes everything better for all that is. You have seen in your science that positive thinking can create geometry, so imagine what it does for you when you are negative.

Negativity is just a state, and when you are aware of it you can change it. First of all, for the to change to occur, you have to forgive yourself and realize that the only person affecting you is you. Forgive yourself, forgive others, and don't let them or their feelings be responsible for how you feel. You are responsible for your own feelings and actions.

Release all the old programming and focus on what really matters—what you know is right. Now is the time for you to forgive yourself and others. Wipe the slate clean and come from a place of love, a new place, a place where you create and affect your own reality, your experience. You are the one you have been waiting for—and it starts with a thought.

Forgive yourself and have compassion and gratitude for your own God Self. Love yourself, and from there you can manifest anything.

November 28, 2014

Shi-Ji via Peter Maxwell Slattery

Chapter 6

THE GOD WITHIN

The veils between worlds are thin at this time, and to go from one world to another there are what you call portals and inter-planes. The Masters know the true nature of non-locality and the true nature of energy and Omnipresence, so they know how to transcend space and time. They use portals that take them to an inter-plane—although all of the inter-planes are actually in the same place between each vibration.

Through some of these portals, you can go from place to place, to other universes, and to the places where the Elohim and other Masters of Light vibrate.

Creator Beings, who are a cell of Source in service mode, set up the solar system and what you call the Milky Way Galaxy. Some of you are these

Beings, and during the creation of the universes some of you personally moved planets, stars, galaxies, and even created them.

With this being said, there is an energy grid set up connecting Orion, Sirius, and The Pleiades. The Orion Council of Light, the Elohim, and The Council of the Whole can be found in different vibrations just behind and above Alnitak (to those in the Southern Hemisphere), although you cannot perceive us there. We also exist just outside your frequency between Sirius A and B, and we exist in the Pleiades between Merope and Electra. Factions of the Elohim and members of The Council of the Whole exist in all these areas, and in other places throughout the universe.

All of the stars in each area of Orion, Sirius, the Pleiades, and other places are not what you perceive them to be. They are not just stars—they are also portals. Each portal also has a gatekeeper, and I am the gatekeeper of the star Merope in the Pleiades.

Metatron is the overseer of all the portals, and all of the portals are connected. The portals that are not stars in Sirius, Orion, and the Pleiades can only be seen and used by those who recognize them. These portals take you to other realms, universes, and beyond.

Only those who have the keys can find and use these portals. These keys can only be obtained by self-mastery and being in service mode. They cannot be given by another being. When you get to the state in which the veil comes down— because you have obtained the keys of knowledge—you will know the location of the portals. This information is in the Book of Knowledge, which will be given to you when you are in a higher state of consciousness.

In the higher state of consciousness, where these planes exist, only those in harmony with them can go there. Connecting to the God within is where all this begins and ends.

Many of you look to Sirius, the Pleiades, and Orion. This is why you have this knowledge on some level. You know the Elohim are in these places, the messengers and creators. You feel the love in these places and there is an energy grid that connects them, affecting everything around, within, and near them. All is connected!

During the history of Earth, many of you have perceived some of the Feline Beings, Bird Beings, Mantis Beings, Reptilians, Nordics, and human-looking Beings as your Gods, but the truth is *you* are all Gods.

Some Beings from these races and others were manipulated by the Lower Light to do certain things to help create hierarchy and structure for the Lower Light. They pretended to be Masters and Gods (even though all is a part of God), to help continue in this vibration: the control for the Lower Light.

You are God and you can do anything, and in becoming human you have taken on the hardest role. Since you are more spiritually advanced than most, you can handle the human experience better than most.

The only reason that you cannot go to the highest of realms now is because of the level of consciousness you are vibrating at while in the body computer. You are here to help change this.

That which you perceive as being the matrix is only a small part of the whole matrix. Only those who have ascended have witnessed the entire matrix, although some of you have had a glimpse of it, when unbounded.

This is where everything starts to unfold for all as a collective. All have access to it! When you truly know that no judgment exists, that the God within is where all is, and that you are loved unconditionally, then can you start to tap into God within you.

You have been led to this and understand it. You are manipulators of space and time; you are remote viewers like nothing else can be; you are the ones the rest are watching and relying on. Because of your lessons, experiences, knowledge, and abilities, because of the call that was made, and because you responded and actually came here, you are the bravest and best suited for the experience of amnesia while in the human body and accomplishing your mission.

Your mission far exceeds this galaxy, this universe, and the other universes. It is part of something so big that even we cannot perceive it in our state.

What we do know is that the change is happening on a mass scale like never seen before. It cannot be fully understood yet, because we are trying to understand the greater intelligence that encompasses our universe, and also other universes. Even in the other realms, we are still learning.

You can gain the keys of knowledge through yourself, your own God Self. You know this already, but we are just reminding you.

The Lower Light is trying to divert you from your true teachings by putting distractions in your way with false prophets and misinformation. The funny thing about this is that it was agreed upon by Source, from how we understand the true nature of reality, but it is a self-mastery exercise with how you react.

Even those who are playing out the Lower Light's agenda in your realm on Earth believe the stories about why they do what they do, as told to them by the Masters of the Lower Light. But deep down, they know what's going on, just like you do. It's just that at this time their body computer is in the mind and not connected to the heart, which, in turn, means they are not connected to the God within at this time.

Instead of their intent coming from their hearts, it's coming from their minds. Their mind chatter is guiding them.

Also, because of the vibration of most here—and due to being in the mind—fear, greed, and what others think are how many run their experience. When coming from the heart you do not do this.

Some people believe their mind chatter is where information comes from, where Guides connect, the higher self-connects, and other Beings connect. They connect in your mind, which you perceive to be your thoughts. Just be aware that the Lower Light can do this to you. You can tell the intention of another by how loving and in service mode the thoughts are.

If you take the time to clear your mind, you can connect with your Guides by noticing your thoughts. Before doing this, tell anything of a self-serving nature that it is not welcome, and that anything coming from a place of service mode is welcome. This can block the Lower Light and connect you to your Guides on an astral and sometimes, body computer level.

Most say they can't meditate because they are unable to clear their mind; however, the truth of the matter is that a lot of the time you don't need to. Take notice of your thoughts, instead. In doing so, you can astral travel, remote view, and go anywhere. With this intent, another consciousness can connect with you and download information to you, or appear astrally or in the physical and communicate with you.

Even old friends and family from the Star Nations and other Beings or other facets of yourself can connect with you. They recognize your soul signature and intention, which can be easily picked up. It's like seeing a blinding light because of their connection to you.

Thoughts bring the information. You might think it's your thoughts, but sometimes (when receiving information) you are interacting with your higher self or your Guides, who are other facets of you, or your family and friends from other planes of existence.

You might think you reincarnate, but you do not. A different facet of your higher self (which is a cell of Source) experiences everything simultaneously. All is a part of God, so strive to connect with the God within.

At this time, many coming into your life, or appearing mysteriously, are those you are connected with on other planes. Some you work nightly in other planes, and then you come back here and work together in many different ways. Some call these Beings Starseeds, the space family, your family, and in a way they are. Although all is one, you are catching up.

In 2010, much was activated, because the waves of Beings who came here and who had been lying dormant woke up slowly. From 2010 to 2012, the energy built up enough to allow a larger portion of the collective in your plane to wake up. This continues at a fast rate.

You might have noticed that since 2012, what you perceive as the common man can now see the corruption from the government more than ever. Many of those who pretended to be in service mode in high government and corporate positions, and even what you call celebrities, are not what they seem.

This happened, and continues to happen, because of the new energies that are helping to wake people up—and because those who are in *self-service* mode were (and are not) coming from their own hearts. As a result, the Lower Light has been working through them. The Lower Light has used and is using all outlets, including government, media, big pharma, and celebrities, as examples of how they want the masses to act and behave. They want all to contribute to their energy source, which they so dearly need to continue, and which is holding everyone back from evolving.

Moving onwards, more will wake up and the baggage of the collective here will come out and be played out, and eliminated. This must happen for the healing of the Earth and humanity, and also for the universe and beyond.

All this will unfold and go in a new direction quickly. It is already in play, and more has already happened than most think. Know it is working.

Some who have been trapped here for a long time have split up their spirit. They have broken away from the manipulation that once held them back, and they have now gone to the New Earth. This should have happened long ago. It has happened everywhere else, in a way, because these other places did not experience manipulation like here on Earth.

With this said, some of you need to stay here because you must hold the energy here until all stabilizes. Then you can pass over. But even then, some of you will stay because you will be the teachers and Guides for those left behind, those who are not ready to evolve at this time. Who evolves and who does not is not so important, because there is no right or wrong way to evolve.

Many have spoken of the New Earth, and they expected this to happen in 2012. Please understand that it has already happened and is continuing to happen.

Most of the groundwork has been done. Now is the time to consciously evolve and tap back into a higher level of consciousness.

All cultures and races need to connect with the God within, not just on Earth but also throughout all planes. This is where it all starts: with you. Everything is up to you.

November 29, 2014

Shi-Ji via Peter Maxwell Slattery

Chapter 7

CREATE YOUR OWN REALITY

Now more than ever, it is time to create your own reality. It is all up to you to create the kind of world you want, the life you want, and the people you surround yourself with. It's all up to you— nobody else. Nothing is out of reach when you come from a place of love with pure intent.

With the new energies coming through, there is no chance for the old ways and baggage to go on. The new vibrations will not allow the old ways to continue. This is just the way it is. Even though will some stay and some will go, both places hold a higher vibration.

With the new energies, all that has been withheld will be known. The people will see everything for what it is. This started before 2010, and then in 2012 it started to set in. And it continues.

Many protest and sign your forms, although these things don't manifest the real change. They are cosmetic in nature. The Lower Light created them in your realm as an illusion to make you think you are creating true change. But the real change starts within—from within you can create any reality you desire. Practicing love, kindness, compassion, affirmations, prayer, and meditation will help in creating your realities, because in these states (and with these acts) you can heighten your vibration. And this, in turn, will help you to connect to your own God Self. This will connect you with the new program, which is also an illusion. All is an illusion, and it's up to you to create the program you want. All programs affect other programs, and the collective.

The old ways cannot exist with the new energies, so be prepared for many issues to come up and be dealt with. Some of you will experience much pain in doing this, but recognize that it will take you to the next level.

On another level, The Council of the Whole (which encompasses all of the Councils) is working with you. They are assisting you in awakening to the knowledge of *who you really are*.

Although there are Light Workers, Angels, Ascended Masters and Councils, the many mansions of God are not limited to any specific number, because God is unbounded. No stone goes unturned—all is loved and accepted by Source.

At this time, the Council of Nine is helping with the programming and adjusting the new energies. They are monitoring the changes that have and are occurring, and will continue to do so. Know you are not alone on any level.

With this being realized, know we are in a war zone in this solar system and humanity is in the middle of it.

As the new energies come in and continue to do so, and because you are close to getting to the galactic plane (which just happened in 2012), the effects are still taking place and the Lower Light is feeling it, too. With these changes comes resistance!

Those who were over-shadowed by the Lower Light—going back thousands of years to Atlantis, Lemuria, and before—knew the power in symbolism, knowledge, astrology, and energy. In time, they made a plan to keep this knowledge from the masses. Only a select few, who were to be the chess pieces that the Lower Light overshadows in this realm, had the knowledge to assist the Lower Light in keeping their power and control.

The Lower Light has taken ancient symbols and manipulated them and their energies in order to contribute to their way. At this time, many are recognizing this.

As we are going through the pivotal point of the change and upgrade of humanity and the universe, the Lower Light is pulling out every trick and weapon, because they are losing their grip on control and power. As they realize their ways, they are breaking up into factions. Take notice of the energies in the coming times.

They do rituals and sacrifices on certain dates, and these dates are known (there are too many to mention here). When they do these rituals and sacrifices, they occur on dates and at times when the energies on the galactic and inter-dimensional levels are strong. They manipulate the energies for the outcome they want to create. Knowing that humans are multidimensional Beings, they

⌐ how energies can contribute in a multidimensional way from humans to their agenda through rituals.

Take notice of the dates when certain events unfold, and you will see they correlate with many Jewish, Christian, and Muslim Holy days. The true stories and meaning of these particular days have been manipulated and changed from their true meanings—and it all has to do with energy.

Events such as New Year's and Christmas are part of this, too! Everyone who celebrates these events is giving energy to the Lower Light. They go with the flow like sheep and contribute their energy to the Lower Light, because of the belief system of so many. They don't know the real meaning behind these dates.

Knowing all this, don't let it be where your focus lies. Just beware of the significance of these dates so you can understand why things are done the way they are. Understand that everything is being manipulated, and also that you can change it, because everything is a projection of our collective reality. Once you know this, you can manipulate it.

The change lies in critical mass. On a body computer 3D level, groups of people holding the same intent can have much more of an effect in this realm with these energies than on an individual level—although even one confident person, one Being, can do just as much as a group of Beings once he or she is in tune with Source.

Many signs have been left and they are in front of you. They are signposts for you, your tools. You have all the tools you need, although most of you are unaware of them.

You are here on a mission that is similar to a military operation. The mission is not to take over like in a military operation on Earth, but rather to help the human race, the Lower Light, Source, the other Sources, and the overall Super God Source, to evolve, because everything has been held back by what's going on here.

When you came down through the planes to this physical reality and reincarnated, you could not come with full knowledge and past life experiences, because of the body computer and the way the body computer brain works. Long ago, we left signs in place, mainly in symbolism and geometry, at what you perceive as ancient sites.

Sacred geometry holds a lot of information for you. Some of you will understand it, but some will not. At the subconscious and energetic levels, it affects all of you.

The Lower Light long ago understood what it was up against, because it once was part of the Creator Beings (the Elohim). The Lower Light knew that the advancement in technologies, media, and more would be what it is today, and it has used and manipulated everything in accordance with their agenda. This is why and how the operation on our end had to happen. We had to be here at this time to help all realize the illusion of karma on a spiritual level, and to help with the process of gaining knowledge and having experiences in all places, not just here.

Slowly, you are all being led to your signs! Look for synchronicities. Notice your thoughts, because this is how consciousness and those you work with in the other realms are guiding and helping you—which you asked them to do in the first place on a higher level.

Some of you will be guided to crystals to start with, and you will continue to use selected ones. Crystals can help activate you and amplify your mission. Some crystals have great powers, but remember that your true power lies within you as your own God Self. Crystals are just to assist you, like your Guides do. This is all!

Sounds and frequencies can help, too. All of you have gifts and you use them on a conscious level occasionally as healers. You use many different types of methods, although only some methods work when you receive a healing done by your fellow Star Brothers and Sisters, because some of you have blockages or you have received implants from self-serving beings.

Try different methods and go with what works. Blockages are part of the program, and sometimes they have been put in place for a reason. With meeting, networking, and healing one another, you also strengthen the energy grid. Everyone you have come across, and all you have done, has been preplanned on another level. In the true profound nature of reality, everything has already happened and the outcome is amazing!

Consciousness is condensed to manifest light, which is then condensed further to make sound, and then still further to make physical matter. All is consciousness. Anything is possible when coming from the heart, from a place of love and good intent.

At this point, you might be asking, "Why is everything the way it is now?" Well...the answer is because just like relationships, it takes two to tango, as your people say! Yes, all is one, but when leaving Source everything still has an individual aspect, even though it is a part of the whole. All humans have had different experiences resulting in different programming, and this is why we are all different.

It's time to connect within, because here everything can change. The answers are available with the help of those behind the scenes. Now more than ever, you are noticing changes in your body, from flutters in your cells to ringing in the ears.

Some of these things are happening because we are communicating with you, and some are commandments from your higher self to your body computer. These commandments change your makeup to get you ready. They change your vibration slowly, because it has to be done slowly in order for the body computer not be damaged. These are some of the shift symptoms. All of you are going through this. Light codes are also being activated. Everything is a code, and everything that is being done is activation. Many activations are happening, from light code activations to physical activations involving your makeup.

Also some of you have energetic implants that can amplify, activate, and assist you through these changes. Some of them help you connect to the spiritual realm. Some of you might think you have one or more of these implants, and you do. Trust what comes to mind first on all this, because that is where the true answer lies.

Your light body is being activated. In turn, your human body is being activated and going back to what it was originally, which is its true nature. You can do anything from levitation to teleportation, to telepathy. You have abilities that many Beings in their physical state do not have to the extent you do, because you have many traits from the advanced Beings from many vibrations. You encompass traits of all the highly advanced Beings, including the Elohim.

You are truly amazing and wonderful, but don't get carried away, because all is equal and all is a cell of God.

Spend time connecting and talking to your physical body—also talk and connect with your light body. Walk barefoot on the Earth and do earthing / grounding exercises to connect with the Earth. Connect with the sun, the planets, the galaxy, the universe, and beyond through your thoughts. Take notice of your feelings and what comes into your mind when doing so.

Connect with your complete self, your higher self, the real you, the "All that is" part. From there you can manifest anything.

November 30, 2014

Shi-Ji via Peter Maxwell Slattery

Chapter 8

SOME STAY, SOME GO

Everything is about evolving, having experiences, and learning our lessons within Source. It's your own illusion, and it's up to you as to how you evolve and when you go on to the next experience—although they are all happening at the same time.

Humans think in a linear way. This was instilled in you through the manipulation. The truth is you can be deprogrammed and create a new program, one in which time is non-existent. Yes...you will age, and yes there are cycles of the planets and so on, although all of it is an illusion.

The illusions are programs, and it's up to you to decide on your program. It's up to you to decide when to move on! There is no right or wrong way to go about your experiences and journey within

Source, because it has to be completely different from everyone else, or else it would not be worth doing. We went out within ourselves (Source) in the first place to gain knowledge and have experiences in as many ways as possible, in order to gain knowledge.

To be effective in your mission here, and to be in prime condition to do what you are here to do, there are many things that need to be in balance.

Nutrition: Be careful about what you put into your bodies. Fruit and vegetables are the best source of foods because they are natural and have a high vibration. Occasionally, a bit of chicken or seafood is okay, and a steak on occasion can help with grounding—although it's best to avoid meat, if possible. Until you are ready to go raw (which is the ultimate goal), do the best you can and don't forget to drink plenty of water.

Water: You can energize your water before drinking it by placing your hands over it and giving it love. You can also blast your water with golden white light using your thoughts. This will also help your body computer. You can also use this method with your food. Health is very important.

Exercise: In addition to eating good food, exercise is important. Whether walking or working out, it's up to you. Keeping the body active is best for your mind, body, and spirit, because sometimes when you exercise you will have thoughts come in as you daydream and go into another state of consciousness, a trance-like state.

Don't overdo it with exercise. Do about twenty minutes of exercise at least six days a week and keep it constant. Don't make it a chore. Do something you actually like doing (whether weights or hiking). Whatever kind of exercise you choose, make it enjoyable.

These tips and tools are to help you be even more effective in doing what you came here to do in a positive and constructive manner. With health, nutrition, and exercise, comes work.

We do not mean work in your usual five-sense Earth world reality way; rather, we mean doing your life's mission and what makes you feel good when you are in service to others. The more of you who are in service doing what you are good at, the more it will benefit all that is.

Each of us has something we are good at, and if we step away from "I can't," and adopt the "Yes I can" attitude, along with it will come all that you need to get by.

The other planes where you have been before operate in a similar way, because in all the places that are a part of the Star Nations, everyone does what they are naturally good at and want to do. They get education and learn about the subjects they are most interested in, and they practice both theory and practical application. Also, if they are passionate about something but have not done it before, they are encouraged to learn and be educated, in order to discover whether they can do what they are passionate about in whatever format they choose.

Learning is very important in all lives, because this is part of what you are meant to do. Always be willing to evolve and not get stuck in the same place, because you will stunt, limit, and slow down your development. These are things you already know because you came from Source to the higher planes, and then to here. We are just reminding you of these things.

Money and finances are the main things that stop people from evolving and doing what they have chosen to do at a higher level while on Earth, along with the "What if" attitude. This attitude was installed in the program here by the Lower Light long ago to keep you trapped and limit your progress. It continues to serve the Lower Light's purpose of keeping you down, which is necessary because you are their energy source. The truth is all is an illusion.

At the end of the day, bills will be paid and your needs will be provided for, including food, clothing, and a roof over your head. If not, a chain of events will happen to make you take new actions and a new direction, which is the path you are meant to be on, and which you have agreed to. You will always have what you need.

As long as you are positive—even though, at times, the human mind will make you worry— know that your Guides, Angels, and the Beings that you work with from beyond are here to help you, calm you, and guide you. All you have to do is ask for their help and then take notice of your thoughts and synchronicities. In time, with them guiding you and showing you the path and the directions to take (which again you have pre-planned and asked for), you will do what you are meant to.

Know you will always be looked after, and that everything will be easier when you do what you are meant to. Whether it's healing, writing, educating, teaching, or performing service, as long as you love and are passionate about what you are doing and you are not hurting anyone, you will have what you need. If you are not certain what you are meant to be doing, ask your Guides and the universe with intent and soon the path will open.

Everything in your life needs to come into balance, including time with friends and family.

You also need a balance of time with your partner or partners. In the Pleiades, Orion, and elsewhere, jealousy does not exist like it does here and acceptance of many partners is normal, unless you are married. Many different types of marriages are agreed to elsewhere, including having children. These marriages are self-regulated, in order to be wanted on both sides, and under the right circumstances for the civilization.

There needs to be a balance in all that you do. Also, having hobbies and time alone is necessary. Most people don't like to be alone, because it makes them think too much. However, being alone is needed to evolve. Contact on many levels can happen consciously by thought, even though everyone has had contact on some level, even if they are not aware of it.

Women in your world tend to have it harder than men because they spend time looking after everyone else, when, actually, everyone should be helping each other.

Women deserve the right to have time by themselves and time with friends, family, social time, and hobbies, just like men. This is more important than ever during the early years when they have children. Later, when the children are older and leave home, they can continue to be on their journey and be Guides to the young ones, even though the young ones are really the Guides to their elders. Many of you are meeting up and having children here (the Starseeds), and this creates a new energy for Beings higher than yourself to come in.

Some of you will get married, some will not. Regarding divorce, it should be understood that in the Star Nations there is an equivalent to a separation between a man and women when they are married, although it is not like here. On Earth, there can be fights, arguments, and more; whereas, elsewhere it is understood that sometimes relationships and people are meant to be together in order to bring certain Beings into the world or do a certain project together.

Sometimes, people have to move on and continue their journey alone. Nothing is a waste of time; it's all part of the journey. Jealousy, control, harm, and emotional and violent abuse are common on Earth. The Lower Light set up this type of energy and it goes right into their grid. Be like the Star Nations in relationships and accept your partner's ex-spouses if they have any. Accept their decisions, be happy, and move on. If kids are involved, hold their highest good as your goal, set boundaries, and avoid jealousy. Be Guides to each other; this is how it is elsewhere.

Coming from a new vibration, the things that once mattered will matter no more, because you are coming at it from a higher level of consciousness. In many places, people have many lovers, not for the sake of it, rather because of a spiritual and sacred connection. Having many partners is not a right; it's a privilege. And like everything else, this cannot be abused.

At this time, many Twin Flames are connecting with each other, and after a certain point, nothing can break them apart, except for themselves. Sometimes when the energies come together again, a lot of issues come up for both partners. This is necessary in order to create new energies and get into harmony with the new program.

At the moment, now more than ever, you are connecting with Beings you have worked with before, old flames you have been with before, and those you are working with on other planes at the same time. You are also connecting with your family from beyond. There is nothing like connecting and being with your Twin Flame. Many Twin Flames are connecting, becoming one whole and ascending together, while bringing in line the male and female energies.

To evolve and be productive in your mission, quiet time and meditation are needed. Whether it's doing deep meditation or just sitting, walking, or standing barefoot on the ground for five minutes a day—away from society, phones, computers, and people, while trying not think—take what quiet time you can. During this time, take notice of your thoughts, because your Guides from beyond can come through (even though they are always there).

Fun is also needed for balance. From this vibration, many Beings from beyond who are in line with you can come through, just from you having fun while holding the intention to connect. So be playful and take notice.

With regard to your friends, family, and acquaintances, not all these people are meant to be in your life forever. Some will teach you lessons, and sometimes these lessons will be about you having self-respect. If those around you (family or not) make you feel bad in a way that's not productive—like bringing up your old baggage or trying to fit you into their program—move on. Their problems are not your problems.

Why be with people who make you feel bad. Take Yeshua (Jesus), for example. Do you really think he wants to come back and interact with those who are praising him and thinking of him with negative feelings as if he is still on a cross, or do you think he would like to be with people who are fun to be around and see him as an equal? Those of you who have interacted with Yeshua know he has a loving, blissful, and happy personality and energy. Happiness in each life is all everyone wants. It it starts with a thought and by connecting with the God within. You can manifest happiness into your reality.

Enjoy your holidays when you get the chance, and work hard within reason; create balance in all you do. Have your goals, vison boards, and connect and go where the signs and synchronicities lead you. Understand that wherever you go on your mission, it will be where you are meant to be. Many will stay to teach the rest and help them evolve, and some of you will go on to be Guides on the New Earth (which has already happened). Also, some will go home and some will ascend. All will go where they are supposed to, including you.

December 1, 2014

Shi-Ji via Peter Maxwell Slattery

Chapter 9

THE NEXT PHASE AND THE NEW BEGINNING

Your next phase is a new beginning. Everything you do fulfils your life purpose, so you don't need to know it while you are doing it.

Even if you feel like you are not doing what you are meant to do, your actions are leading you to your purpose in this realm. Nothing goes to waste. In this facet of your oversoul, whatever you do is your mission.

Learning, gaining knowledge, and having experiences is the true blueprint and foundation of why we lose ourselves, only to find ourselves again within Source.

Just know that the way to change or achieve anything is by thought. As long as your thoughts are in service mode and your intentions are pure, there will be no repercussions to worry about, because you are unconditionally loved by Source and there will be no judgment.

With the next phase and realization of all you have read in this book, how to proceed is up to you. All of you reading this are being changed on some level. How you change will come into play in many ways. Remember, nothing goes unnoticed, and no one is more important than anyone else. All is equal. Everyone is playing a part in human evolution at this time. All of us are different and what we do is different.

As the new energies come in, so are other spirits in the reincarnation process, although reincarnation (as we have mentioned) does not exist. The new spirits resonate well with the new energies, because they are from the higher planes and they are already adapted to it.

Please take special notice of the kids. Pay attention to the kids. Many doctors and specialists are talking about how kids have attention deficient disorder, Asperger's or autism, and many other diagnoses. The truth of the matter is that they are using a different part of their brain. They need more to do, because they are very active, and because they are reacting differently to the body computer. The kids are operating at a high vibration.

As many of you already know, you are not from here, and how things are done here is slow. This is part of the self-mastery lesson. The kids will have a bigger lesson to learn because they are from the higher planes and they are more evolved. However, they can do it. The kids are really our teachers.

The kids are developing much more quickly than those of you who are adults. They are solving problems and learning, and they see things for what they are more quickly than adults. The main change that is going to happen here will come from the kids.

Many Starseeds don't want kids, even though this is where the change starts and where the energy comes from (the kids have high energy). These days, the kids need to be tested and given things to pull apart and put together, because there are not enough challenges for their high intelligence.

Learn from the kids—they are your teachers, not the other way around. On every level you will learn! You will learn about yourself, your emotions, your happiness, that all is a projection of you. The kids will show you everything. They will show you other ways to do and think of things, while bringing in the vibe and vibration of happiness.

More now than ever before, the kids are connected to their home stars, their Guides, and their many facets. They are bringing their many traits through to help here. They know we are not alone, and they have a lot more conscious memory of past lives (although our lives are all happening at the same time).

Also, the kids have more conscious memories of their experiences, while in the human body, because they can handle more. It takes a lot to startle them, due to their high vibration.

Ask yourself, "What can I do for the new kids"? This is where the change lies, in addition to working on yourself.

For those who have been stuck here for thousands of years, your time to move on is now—if you want to. It's up to you. The opportunity awaits you, if you want to take it. There is no right or wrong way to go about it. You will know when you are ready. The New Earth is already in existence and there are many there to assist and help you take the next step in your soul evolution. It's your decision.

As you evolve, those who have been stuck here in this plane, and others throughout the universe and beyond, will have the opportunity to evolve and move on to their next experience and lesson, because the road bump that once stopped them no longer exists. The change that is happening now is so big and beautiful.

The main message given to you in this book is know that you are loved and, no matter what, you are special. In the bigger scheme of things, only you can judge yourself. No one else can judge you, because you are God, a cell of God, a part of the collective, which is really one.

Take the time, now more than ever, to work on yourself. Give yourself the best care you can. In this way, you will also be giving your best to those around you in this realm and in all realms, and to Source itself and beyond, because you are a part of a bigger collective than you realize.

Truly, your Masters, Saints, and Sages are real, and they are no better than you. They just happen to be the messengers who have come down through the dimensions to this physical plane in order to help you remember who you are (assuming you want to remember). Whatever they can do, you can do, too, because all of you are Creator Beings.

Now...some of the Beings you interact with are transported in what you might call UFOs, flying saucers, discs, cigar-shaped crafts, or orbs. However, the Creator Beings, the Ascended Beings, and the like, transport themselves in what you call Merkabahs. They travel around in their own light bodies and they are able to do anything or go anywhere just by thinking about it.

You can do this, too, and you have and are doing it on another level at this time, although some of you are not connected to another facet of yourself consciously and you are unaware of this. Some of you are connected to other parts of yourself and have a feeling you are a lot more. Only a small majority of you know your true capabilities.

The knowledge of your true self and what you want to be and create is up to you. It's also up to you as to how many facets of yourself will become masters, because all of them can be if you seek it. Intent and service is where it all starts.

Many of you want to know where you're from. The truth is you are from Source. You are God, a cell of God, and you have vibrated through many programs within God to experience all that is. You have been and done many things throughout your journey.

Take notice of the stars in the night sky. You have been there and you are there. Not only have you had one lifetime in these places you have had many. You have been many, many, many different types of Beings. The part of yourself you are tapping into now is the life of all lives, and with it comes the experience of all experiences, which is the human experience—and what an experience it is! What an illusion it is, just like everything else except for Source itself, or is Source an illusion, too?

Many who walk among you at this time are not what they seem. Your reality is not what it seems. Most think they are not in control, but they are. The more of you who take control, the easier it will be for others to change their reality and take control.

Many of your Guides are walking among you. Some are extraterrestrials and some are Masters and Angels, or whatever you would like to call them. The fact is they are among you and have been with you for a long time. You have interacted with them in the past, and you are interacting with them now. To see one, just go and look in the mirror. There you will see a Master, because you are a Master.

First, to realize this, you must love yourself. Forgive yourself for any wrong you believe you have done. Forgive yourself for perceiving separation, the illusion of separation, and forgive yourself for judging others.

Forgive others for any wrong they have done to you (which is also an illusion) and see the lessons. Learn from the lessons and the realization of what we are telling you, which is, "You are the master of your own destiny."

Gods lose themselves and find themselves. This is what all the cells of Source do. It's a cycle. Now is the time for you to find yourself, to fully wake up and take your power back. Realize you are the one in power and that you are here to help, not only others, but yourself, too. This is what happens when helping others.

From now on, take notice of your thoughts, and ask in your mind where they are coming from; ask who sees through your eyes, and you will notice you are connected outside of your body, going to your higher oversoul, and then again going out from that to the state of pure God Consciousness. From there you can go to the Super God Consciousness state, which is what everything is connected to within and outside of the universe.

Heal yourself now, set the intent, forgive yourself, and connect back to yourself like never before. Get rid of the old programs and beliefs, and get with the new program, your program. When you need help, ask your Guides, the Saints, Sages, and Masters, and your higher self for help. Go where the signs lead you. From synchronicities to numbers, to people bringing up the same subjects, take notice because these are signs. Notice the thoughts that come to mind when these things happen. Go with the flow and know everything will be taken care of. You will be taken care of.

Now more than ever, connect with like-minded people. You have already agreed to this. It is time to take your position in the grand plan for healing and awakening the human race.

Those you come across are your Guides, and you are theirs. Support each other. Some of them will fade away and new ones will come into your life, although on some level you are and always will be working together. You are helping each other and teaching each other the necessary lessons.

As a collective and in small groups, through meditation and prayer, you are setting the bar for Oneness. In this way, you can affect your reality on Earth and also on a universal level and beyond in other universes. It all starts with the spark of a flame, your flame, your cell of Source. It all starts with you.

December 2, 2014

Shi-Ji via Peter Maxwell Slattery

FINAL NOTE

Make of this what you may and interpret it as you may.

Cheers, love, and light,

Peter Maxwell Slattery

GLOSSARY

Aboriginal (Original Person – preferred name for Aboriginals) Masters – Ascended Aboriginal or Aboriginal who has obtained spiritual enlightenment and is in service to Earth and Source.

Akashic records – A place / realm where all events throughout all planes and dimension are held and knowledge accessible to all.

(the) Archons (the Lower Light) – Part of the Elohim that stayed within Source and did not go back to their God state. They are the force stopping all Beings from connecting back to Source; they attempt to control and keep supremacy over all. They are also created an Artificial Intelligence that harvests negative energy; they run on negative energy and feed off negative energy and events from the human race and all beings; this keeps them in existence.

Ascended Master – Spiritually enlightened Beings who obtained enlightenment after many incarnations and are now in service to humanity, the earth, the universe, and Source.

Astral, astral travel – Leaving the body in energy / conscious form and travelling the universe and its planes and dimensions.

Atlantis and Lemuria – Two previous civilizations on Earth that were Pleiaidian Colonies.

Bases – A facility that is run, owned, and operated by branches of extraterrestrial groups or races, or by humans or military, as a command center or outpost. Bases shelter crafts and have equipment and research facilities, manage operations, and store supplies.

Being(s), Ancient Beings (spirit beings, but also used here for human beings) – ET Beings, Light Beings, humans, anything that has consciousness.

Being of Light – Conscious Being structured from light.

(other) Beings: Feline Beings, Bird Beings, Mantis Beings, Nordics, and human-looking Beings – humanoid type conscious Beings with traits of an Earth human, but can have different features.

Book of Knowledge – Book that holds knowledge and wisdom in all areas and subject matters.

Brotherhood of Light – Highly evolved spiritual conscious Beings who can assume any form; they are responsible for holding order throughout the universe for Source. They pave the way and also hold space for civilizations to evolve.

(the) Council of the Whole – A Council with the job of regulating all within Source and bringing balance.

(the) Council of Nine – A group of advanced light beings who are teachers and regulators for the evolution of the universe; they assist all councils.

(Orion) Council of Light – A spiritually advanced group of Beings that regulate and assist the Orions and also other races.

Craft(s) – Commonly referred to as UFOs / spacecrafts – Some are structured with exotic materials; others are Light vehicles (Merkabah) structured from consciousness and light. Some are grown and are organic. Crafts are trans-dimensional, able to time travel and breach the speed of light, and can have consciousness themselves.

Crop circles — Geometrical formations found mainly in farmers' field / crops; they carry messages and information. Mainly done by extraterrestrials on Earth and other advanced civilizations, although some are faked by Earth humans or military to make the masses think there is nothing to them.

3-D Level — The third density, or dimension, that humans are experiencing at this time.

(the) Elohim (also known as Anunnaki) — The First Beings that manifested on planetary bodies in physical form that were not female or male. "Anunnaki" also means those who came to Earth from the heavens, as described in ancient Sumerian text; another name for the Original Lyrans that came into being in the Elohim state.

Experiencer — Someone who has had or is having experiences of what is deemed to be paranormal experiences or contact with another form of supernatural intelligence (the supernatural and paranormal are actually normal).

Extraterrestrials, E.T.s — Intelligences from elsewhere in the universe and beyond; not from Earth.

(the) Fallen Ones – a term from the Bible referring to the Archons (the Lower Light); the Elohim that left source and did not stay in their God state; they manipulate and create negative energy so they can stay and exist.

Gaia – Another name for Earth.

Gatekeeper – A Being who is responsible for and protector of a dimensional gate / stargate, or portal, that allows access to and from other places and realms.

(the) Guardians – Those that protect and defend, regulate and monitor all that is.

Guide(s) (spirit guides) – An entity or Being that is not incarnated in a physical body, and that is protecting or guiding humans during the human experience. Sometimes they are extraterrestrial; they can also be other facets of the consciousness of the person who perceives them as a guide from another realm / dimension.

Inter-planes – The planes between dimensions / densities; all inter planes are in the same place, dimension.

Light Being, Light Cities – Beings with consciousness structured from light or cities structured from light.

Merkabah: (Light Vehicle) – Created from an individual Being's light body / consciousness that can be trans-dimensionally travelled in.

Metatron – Worker Being for Source, who is the Master of the Electron, regulating all thought, consciousness, movement, through all planes and dimensions and is everywhere at once through the Electron.

Michael – Worker Being for Source; a protector Being who regulates all that is; works in synch with Metatron and can also be everywhere at once.

Nephilim – Hybrid, part ET or otherworldly being, and part human.

New Earth – A new vibrational frequency of Earth; those who have elevated their level of consciousness can start to experience and perceive the New Earth. Some can shift into the frequency; this New Earth is right beside the frequency you are now experiencing.

Orb – Can appear as a ball of light and has consciousness; orbs can be an E.T., spirit, nature spirit, elemental, fairy, bigfoot, and many other types of intelligences. Some appear in their natural form, or they can appear as one, or it can be a by-product before a Being appears in physical form. Also, some are monitoring devices, a drone, or a Merkabah of a Being. An orb is basically an intelligence that is trying to explode from another frequency into your reality.

Oversoul – Your higher self, your Elohim self, which is a cell of Source.

Portals – Gateways and transporter to other places, realms.

Remote viewing – Being able to perceive anywhere in space and time, local or non-local or non-linear.

Reptilians – Humanoid beings of many different types and shapes and sizes. They work with the Archons to control the human races, although some are seeing their ways and changing due to not being able to evolve in consciousness (because they are in service to self and the lower light).

OTHER HUMANOID BEINGS:

Jinn – Supernatural Beings that are either in self-service mode or they are trickster Beings that are not positive or negative; they can appear in any form if they wish to do so.

Greys – They come in many different colors, but mainly grey; they are the typical aliens people hear about with the big, black, almond-shaped eyes; they are skinny and have big heads. They come from many places; some were once human and some are androids. Some are in service to humanity or other forces; they can be of a positive or negative nature.

Shadow Beings – They appear as shadows in humanoid form; they are mainly in self-service mode or they are working for the Lower Light.

Mantis Beings (Insectoids) – One of the most ancient races in the universe; they are mainly mediators and scientific in nature; they look like mantis' or part humanoid and part mantis; they come in many sizes and colors.

STARS AND CONCELLATIONS:

Sirius – Binary star system.

Pleiades – Star Cluster.

Orion – Star Constellation.

Arcturus – Giant red star located in the constellation Boötes.

Lyra – A relatively small constellation.

Alnitak – One of the three stars in Orion's Belt.

Andromeda – A constellation and also there is the Andromeda galaxy.

Merope, Electra – Stars in the Pleiades.

Sirians, Orions, Pleiadians/Plejarens – Beings from Sirius, Orion, and Pleiades that come in many different forms, shapes, sizes, and colors.

Star Family (star traits) – Family you have had past experiences with, or from where you have once incarnated (although all lives are being experienced at the same time).

Starseed – Someone who has has lived in other ET civilizations.

Star Nations Galactic Councils, Federation – Names for the collective groups of ET races that are at unity but still respect each other's ways, basically an ET United Nations. They exist to uphold order and balance between the ET races.

(the) Temple – The human body.

Third Eye – Energy center in the human energy body, associated with the pineal gland, which is located basically in the middle of the human brain. It is an antenna and receiver for visuals, and can also can be used to communicate through visuals to anywhere in space and time with other intelligences.

Twin-Flame – Someone who resonates with you, can be a mirror, is a good balance, can bring balance, and is part of your soul family, which means you have had many missions together and come from the same oversoul, and in some cases, race / soul groups.

UFO – An unidentified flying object.

Walk-in – Another consciousness that can jump into the physical vessel: e.g. the human body, while the original consciousness that was in the body leaves.

Other books by Peter Maxwell Slattery:

The Book of Shi-Ji 2

The Book of Shi-Ji 3

ABOUT THE AUTHOR

Peter Maxwell Slattery is an international bestselling author, and he is known as an ET contact experiencer. His ET experiences started at an early age and continue to this day, with hundreds of witnesses to events. He has an overwhelming amount of photographic and video evidence related to UFOs, otherworldly Beings, and apparitions, plus physical trace evidence.

His experiences with extraterrestrials have led him to help people and groups make ET contact themselves, in addition to healing and tapping into their own abilities. Pete has appeared on Channel 7's *Prime News* and *Sunrise*, and many other television programs internationally. He has made worldwide news, been in numerous documentaries, written about in magazines, and been a guest on mainstream radio shows, including *Coast-to-Coast*. He is also a musician and, as a filmmaker, he has made a number of documentaries on the subject of E.T.s.

Peter Maxwell Slattery continues to open the world up to the greater reality that "We are not alone" and that "We are all amazing, powerful Beings."

For more information go to petermaxwellslattery.com

Follow Pete on Facebook, YouTube Instagram, and Twitter

Made in the USA
Middletown, DE
07 May 2020